Clothes We Wear

Written by Joanna Pascoe

Illustrated by Gustavo Mazali

School uniform

School children wear a uniform.

Spring and summer clothes

The weather is warm in spring. It's hot in summer.

Autumn and winter clothes

The weather is cool in autumn.

It's cold in winter.

Japanese clothes

Japan is warm in spring.

People wear cool kimonos.

Spanish clothes

Spain has got hot weather in summer.

A flamenco dancer wears a pretty red dress.

Scottish clothes

In Scotland, the weather is cool in autumn.

Men and boys sometimes wear warm kilts.

Siberian clothes

There is snow and ice in Siberia in winter. People wear warm animal furs.

George's Snow Clothes

Written by Joanna Pascoe
Illustrated by Gustavo Mazali

Woof! Woof!
Whoopee! It's snowing.
Let's make a snowman!

Rex looks for George's warm clothes.

What's under the bed?

Good dog, Rex!
Here's my warm hat.
Woof! Woof!

What's in the kitchen?

Rex has got George's orange jumper.

Here are my blue trousers!

Whoops!
I'll take my
hat off first.
Woof!
My coat! Thanks,
Rex. Now, where
are my socks?

Look! My scarf and gloves.
But, where are my socks? I don't want cold feet!

Rex! There are my socks!

Where are George's scarf and hat?

The Snowman

On a cold day,
You can play with snow.
Make a snowman,
Have a go!

The snowman wears a scarf
And a grey hat.
Winter clothes are warm,
We like that!

Activities

1 Colour and label the clothes.

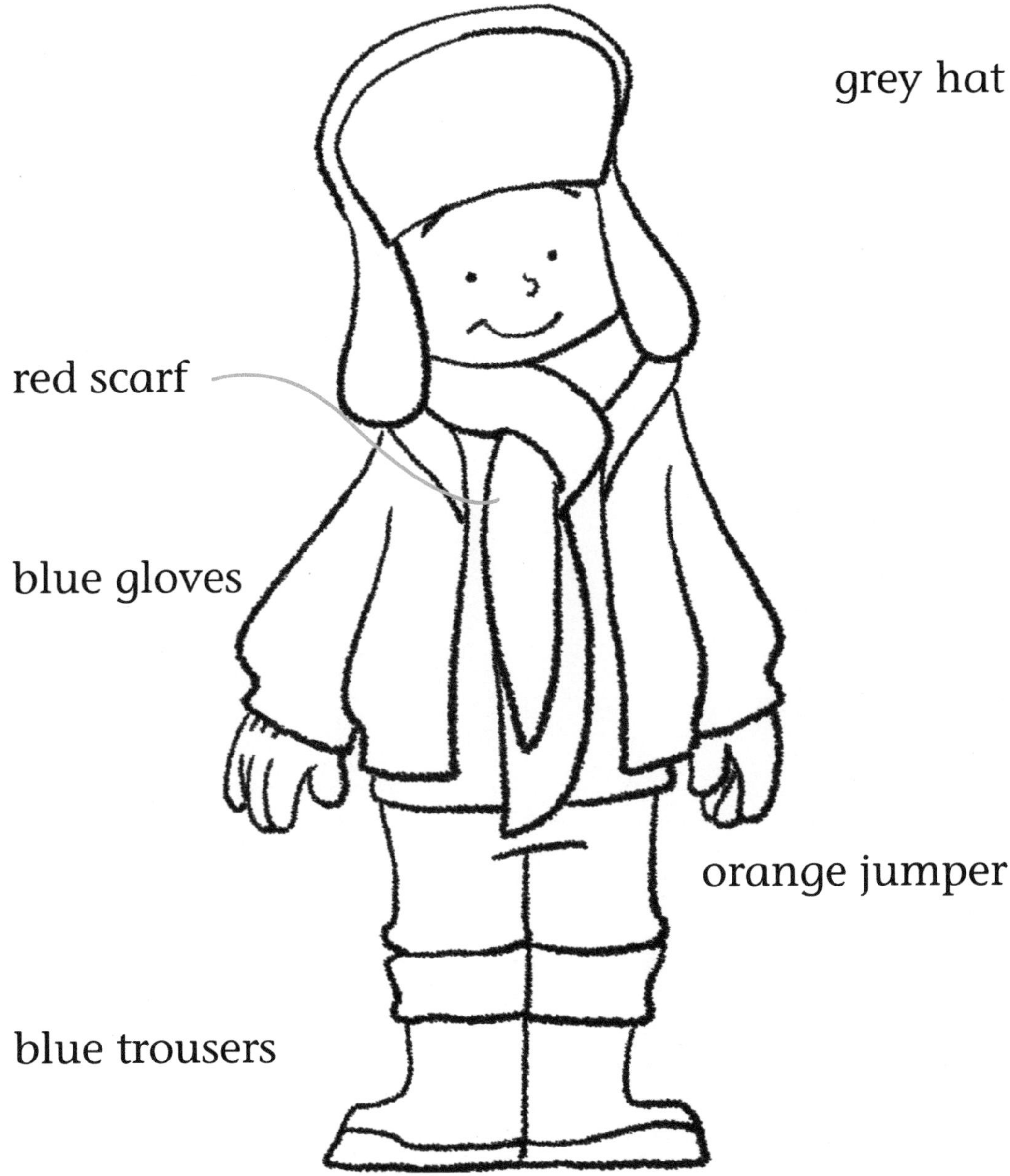

2 Write the word *is* or *are*. Write the number.

Here ___are___ some shorts. [4]

Here ________ a jumper. [ ]

Here ________ a coat. [ ]

Here ________ some socks. [ ]

Picture Dictionary

hat

jumper

trousers

coat

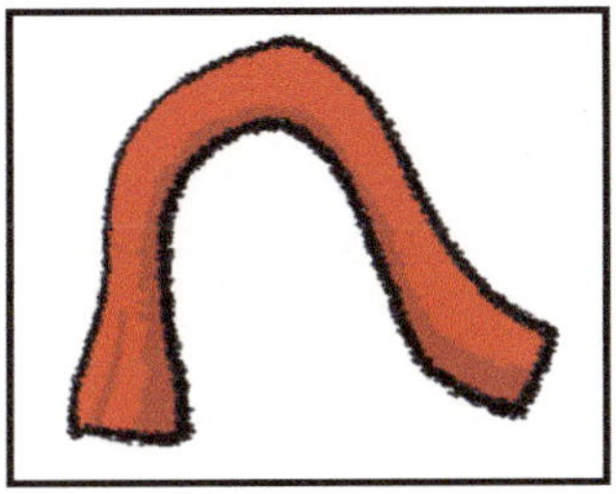
scarf

gloves

socks

snowman

winter

spring

summer

autumn

Macmillan Education
4 Crinan Street
London N1 9XW
A division of Macmillan Publishers Limited
Companies and representatives throughout the world

ISBN 978-0-230-46919-8

Written by Joanna Pascoe

First published 2015

Designed by Carolyn Gibson
Illustrated by Gustavo Mazali
Picture research by Emily Taylor
Cover photograph by **Shutterstock**/Studio Light and Shade

The authors and publishers would like to thank the following for permission to reproduce their photographs: **Alamy**/Craig Holmes Premium p2, Alamy/Losevsky Pavel p4(l), Alamy/Ian Thraves p7; **Alamy Stock Photo**/Sven Hagolani p5(tr); **Corbis**/68/Ocean p4(r), Corbis/Jacques Langevin/Sygma p8; **Getty Images**/kali9 p3, Getty Images/hanapon1002 p5(bl); **ThinkStock/**dmbaker p6.

Printed and bound in Brazil

2025
14